21st Century Junior Library

# SERVICE DOGS

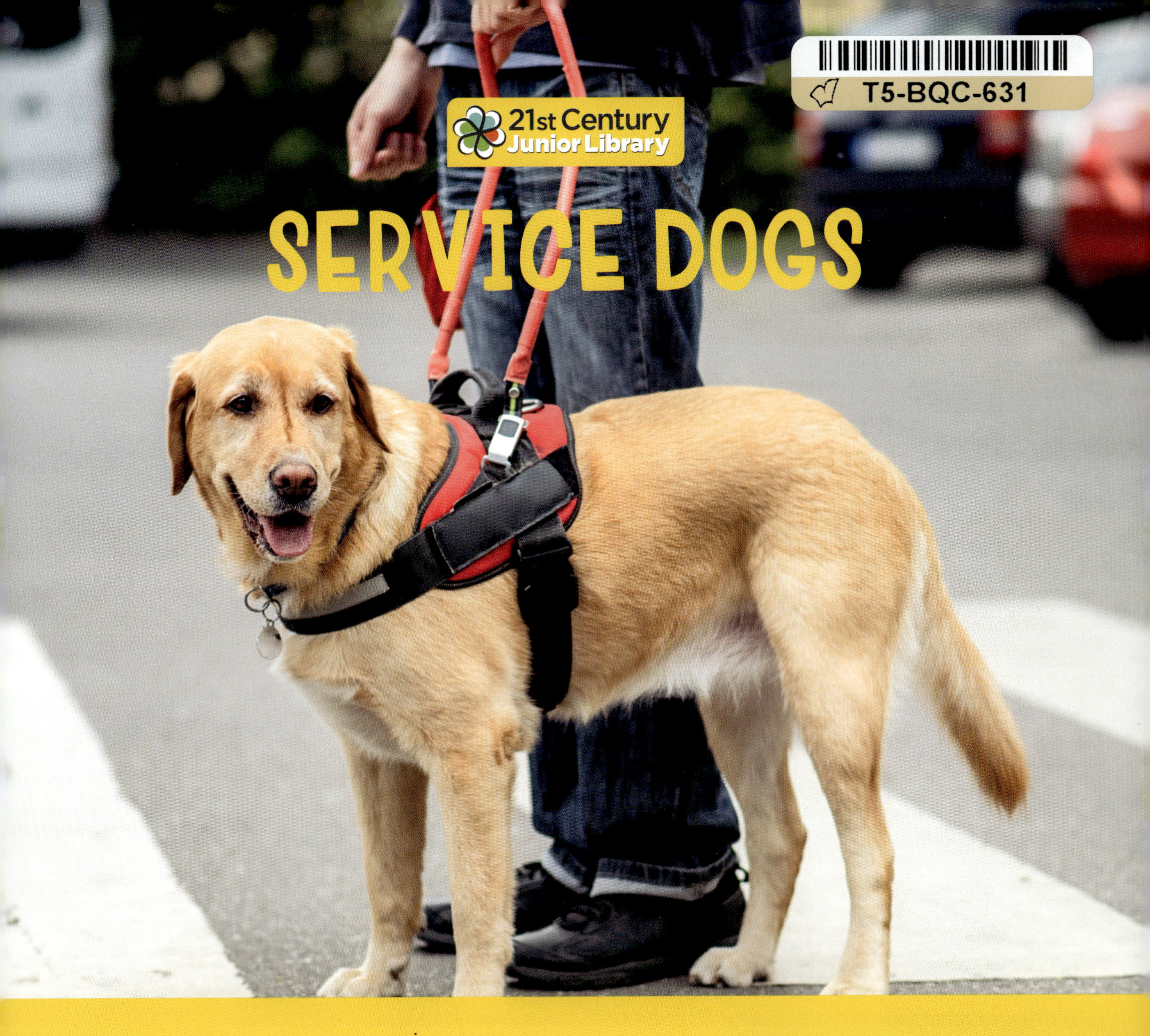

Beth Finke

easterseals

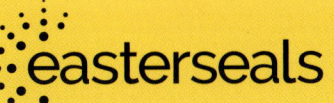

Understanding Disability

Published in the United States of America by:

CHERRY LAKE PRESS
2395 South Huron Parkway, Suite 200, Ann Arbor, Michigan 48104
www.cherrylakepress.com

Reading Adviser: Beth Walker Gambro, MS, Ed., Reading Consultant, Yorkville, IL

Photo Credits: © SasaStock/Shutterstock.com, cover, 1; © Roman Chazov/Shutterstock.com, 5; © Alistair Heap/Alamy Stock Photo, 6; © AnnGaysorn/Shutterstock.com, 7; © Arterra Picture Library/Alamy Stock Photo, 8; © 24K-Production/Shutterstock.com, 9; © WilleeCole Photography/Shutterstock.com, 10, 11; © Shine Caramia/Shutterstock.com, 12; © funkyteddy/Shutterstock.com, 13; © John Dowling/Shutterstock.com, 15; © Design Pics Inc/Alamy Stock Photo, 16; © Anastasiia Marchenko/Shutterstock.com, 19; © XiXiXing/Shutterstock.com, 20

Copyright © 2023 by Cherry Lake Publishing Group

All rights reserved. No part of this book may be reproduced or utilized in any form or by any means without written permission from the publisher.

**Cherry Lake Press** is an imprint of Cherry Lake Publishing Group.

Library of Congress Cataloging-in-Publication Data
Names: Finke, Beth, 1958- author.
Title: Service dogs / by Beth Finke.
Description: Ann Arbor, Michigan : Cherry Lake Publishing, [2022] | Series: Understanding disability | Includes bibliographical references. | Audience: Grades 2-3
Identifiers: LCCN 2022005376 | ISBN 9781668910672 (paperback) | ISBN 9781668909072 (hardcover) | ISBN 9781668912263 (ebook) | ISBN 9781668913857 (pdf)
Subjects: LCSH: Service dogs—Juvenile literature. | People with disabilities—Juvenile literature.
Classification: LCC HV1569.6 .F56 2022 | DDC 362.4/0483—dc23/eng/20220214
LC record available at https://lccn.loc.gov/2022005376

Cherry Lake Press would like to acknowledge the work of the Partnership for 21st Century Learning, a Network of Battelle for Kids. Please visit http://www.battelleforkids.org/networks/p21 for more information.

Printed in the United States of America
Corporate Graphics

Easterseals is enriching education through greater disability equity, inclusion and access. Join us at www.Easterseals.com.

# CONTENTS

Service Dogs and the Law     4

Many Tasks     10

Three Simple Rules     17

     Extend Your Learning     21
     Glossary     22
     Find Out More     23
     Index     24
     About the Author     24

# SERVICE DOGS AND THE LAW

Many breeds of dogs in the United States are trained to help people who have disabilities. The Americans with Disabilities Act (ADA) is a public law that all Americans follow. It defines service dogs as "dogs that are individually trained to do work or perform **tasks** for people with disabilities." That means service dogs are specifically trained to help people with disabilities do things they are unable to do on their own.

Have you ever seen a service dog?

Under the ADA, only dogs can be service animals. In rare instances, **miniature horses** work as service animals and can be in public places with the person they're trained to help.

Service dogs are trained to help calm their handlers. Handlers are the people they have been trained to help.

# Make a Guess!

Would you guess that a lot of people with disabilities have a miniature horse as a service animal? Why do you think miniature horses are allowed to be service animals in special situations? Can you think of one thing miniature horses do better than dogs? How about one trait dogs have that miniature horses don't?

Because service dogs are specially trained, they get special **privileges**. They get to go anywhere the person with the disability goes. Even if a sign says, "No Dogs Allowed," a service dog can go in.

Service dogs help their handlers move through public spaces.

8

However, the service dog has to be **accompanied** by the person they've been trained to help. Service dogs are not allowed to go into a public place by themselves. They only get the special privileges if they are with the person who needs them.

## Ask Questions!

What types of training do service dogs need? Do some research and see if you can find an organization that trains service dogs in your community.

# MANY TASKS

Some service dogs are trained to help people who have physical disabilities. Other service dogs are trained to help people who have mental disabilities. But there's one thing all service dogs have in common. Each one is specially trained to do tasks that a person's disability prevents them from doing on their own. Service dogs can be trained to perform all sorts of tasks for people with disabilities. Here are a few examples:

- **Guide dogs** help people who are blind cross streets, **navigate** spaces safely, and avoid **obstacles**.

# Look!

Keep an eye out for service dogs and their handlers next time you are in public. How do they help the people they assist? What tasks do you see them doing?

Some service dogs wear special vests in public so other people know they working.

- **Hearing dogs** help people who are Deaf by alerting them to important sounds like a baby's cry, an alarm, or a doorbell.
- **Seizure** response dogs get their handlers out of an unsafe space before a seizure so they don't get hurt. Some also learn to bark to alert others that their person is having a seizure.

- **Autism** service dogs help calm their handlers' emotional **distress** with a gentle paw or a soft lean.
- **Mobility assistance** dogs fetch things, press automatic buttons to open doors, carry bags, and can even pull wheelchairs.

# Think!

Comfort pets and emotional support animals aren't allowed into public places that don't allow pets. But service dogs are allowed as long as they are accompanied by their person. Why do you think lawmakers decided not to give comfort pets and emotional support animals the same privileges that service dogs have?

- **Post-traumatic stress disorder** (PTSD) service dogs help their person feel safer by entering a home first to check each room, turning lights on with a foot pedal, and waking their person from nightmares.

Many people like to have a pet with them all the time to keep them calm and make them feel better. These pets are called "comfort animals" or "emotional support animals." They do not qualify as service dogs. Comfort animals make their owners feel better just by being around. Service dogs learn to understand what their person's disability is. They are specially trained to do a job or task when needed.

Service dogs start training when they are puppies.

Service dogs are just as loving as regular dogs.

16

# THREE SIMPLE RULES

Dogs can be hard to resist! If you see a cute dog somewhere, you may want to run up and give them a treat, pet them, or say hello. However, giving that sort of attention to a service dog is not a good idea. Distracting a service dog could put the dog and the person they're helping in a dangerous situation. Imagine a guide dog getting ready to lead their person around a hole in the sidewalk just as someone calls out to offer the dog a treat. The dog turns toward the person with the treat, and crash! The person falls and gets hurt.

You can keep a service dog team safe and show them how much you respect the work they do by following these three simple rules:

- **Rule 1:** Always ask the person working with the service dog if it's alright for you to pet their dog before you start reaching toward the dog.
- **Rule 2:** Don't click your tongue or whistle to get the dog's attention. This might distract them from the task they're doing for their person.
- **Rule 3:** Don't feed service dogs. Service dogs have to stay healthy to do their work. The treat you're offering the dog might make them sick. When a service dog is too sick to work, it leaves the person with the disability without the help they need.

Service dogs do more than just help with everyday tasks. They also become trusted friends of the people who love and need them. Feel free to say hello to the person working with the service dog. You could even add a compliment like, "Nice dog!" or "I love your dog!" Just try your best to avoid talking to the service dog directly. That way, every person—and every service dog—stays safe!

# Create!

**With these three rules in mind, create a poster or slideshow. Share it with friends and family so they can learn the rules about how to keep a service dog team safe.**

# EXTEND YOUR LEARNING

What do you think it would feel like to be a service dog? Choose one type of service dog from the list in the Many Tasks section of the book. Pretend you're a dog with that job. Does your work make you feel proud? Do people smile when they see you out with your person? Is your job hard sometimes? Can you share a story about an especially hard day at work? What about an especially good day at work? What privilege do you have that other dogs don't? Now write a story from a service dog's point of view. Your story can be long or short or a chapter book or a picture book. Be creative!

# GLOSSARY

**accompanied** (uh-KUHM-puh-need) went with a person or thing

**autism** (AH-tih-zuhm) a developmental disorder with a broad range of conditions including challenges with social skills, repetitive behaviors, and speech

**distress** (diss-TRESS) needing help

**miniature horses** (MIH-nee-uh-chuhr HOHR-sez) horses defined by their small height, often only 3 feet (0.9 meters) tall

**mobility assistance** (moh-BIH-luh-tee uh-SIH-stuhns) devices or things that help people move or get around

**navigate** (NAV-uh-gayt) to find a way through

**obstacles** (AHB-stih-kuhls) things that block a person's way or keep them from moving forward

**post-traumatic stress disorder** (pohs-truh-MAH-tik STREHS dihs-OR-duhr) a condition in which people have a hard time recovering after a shocking or frightening event; also called PTSD

**privileges** (PRIV-lij) unearned and sometimes unnoticed advantages

**seizure** (SEE-zhur) a sudden attack of convulsions or unconsciousness, often related to a brain disorder

**tasks** (TASKS) jobs or chores

# FIND OUT MORE

## Books
Davidson, B. Keith. *Service Dog.* New York, NY: Crabtree Publishing, 2022.

Finke, Beth. *Hanni and Beth: Safe & Sound.* West Bay Shore, NY: Blue Marlin Publications, 2007.

Murray, Julie. *Service Animals.* North Mankato, MN: ABDO Publishing, 2020.

## Websites
**Get Involved with Easterseals**
https://www.easterseals.com/get-involved
Learn about the different ways you can get involved in increasing opportunities for people with disabilities, from advocacy to volunteering.

**YouTube—Kids Meet a Guide Dog for the Blind**
https://www.youtube.com/watch?v=PW2duKZChA8
Watch kids meet a guide dog and learn about some of his tasks.

**YouTube—Service Dogs 101**
https://www.youtube.com/watch?v=ZqvW3AabbWI
National Center on Health, Physical Activity and Disability (NCHPAD) shows service dogs at work and explains some of the differences between emotional support animals and service dogs.

# INDEX

Americans with Disabilities Act (ADA), 4, 6
autism service dogs, 13

comfort pets, 13–14

emotional support animals, 13–14

guide dogs, 8, 10, 17

hearing dogs, 12

miniature horses, 6–7
mobility assistance dogs, 13

post-traumatic stress disorder service dogs, 14

public places
  rules about, 7, 9, 13
  service dogs' services, 6–13, 17

respecting service dogs/owners, 17–19
rules
  behavior around service dogs, 17–19
  public spaces and service dogs, 7, 9, 13

safety
  behavior around service dogs, 17–19
  service dogs' offerings, 10–14, 17
seizure response dogs, 12

service animals
  emotional support, 13–14
  miniature horses, 6–7
service dogs
  defined, 4
  identification, 11–12
  laws, 4, 6
  pictures of, 5, 8-9, 11–12, 15-16, 20
  skills of, 4, 8, 10–14
  training, 4, 6–7, 9, 14–15
  treatment of, 17–19
  writing about, 21

training of service dogs, 4, 6–7, 9, 14–15

writing exercises, 21

# ABOUT THE AUTHOR

**Beth Finke** is a writer and the blog moderator for Easterseals National Office. Her picture book about seeing eye dogs, *Safe & Sound*, won an award for children's literature from the American Society for the Prevention of Cruelty to Animals. Beth's seeing eye dog flew on a plane with her to California and guided her on stage to accept that award. When Beth isn't writing books, she likes to teach writing classes, swim, play jazz piano, and go with friends to live concerts and plays. She lives in Chicago with her husband, Mike, who can see, and Luna, a black Lab who guides Beth safely everywhere she needs to go.